Believest

Thou This

By Bill Howard

Believest Thou This

Printed in the United States of America by CREATESPACE

Bible Quotations are noted with their abbreviations: King James Version (KJV), New King James Version (NKJV), New International Version (NIV), New Living Translation (NLT).

Cover and Interior Design by Bradley S. Cobb

ISBN: 978-1508556312

Foreword

As beauty is in the eye of the beholder so will the efficacy of this writing be judged by the effect upon the reader, whether that number be few or many. The most likely first question that will come to mind is: *Why another book based on spiritual principles?* The words of our God are so many and so meaningful that any attempt to reach one who does not yet comprehend is worthy of any effort. The writer can say joyfully that he has experienced a wonderful life with innumerable blessings, but in the same sentence admit to many failures and shortcomings. By the grace of God, he has been allowed four score and four years on this earth. Whatever God has in mind beyond that is in question. This work then will be written with a prayerful spirit and a deep-seated hope that those who follow after me will read and comprehend what I have tried to set forth as unquestionable truths from God's own words.

Dedication

As always, contemplating the thoughts that make up the dedication of a book, I think first of my loving, patient and helpful wife, Juanita, without whose help and encouragement and careful eye to catch my mistakes, I would not be writing. To a beautiful family with which God so generously blessed me, I express my love and appreciation. For the times I have failed, I ask forgiveness. Our blended family consists of eight children, sixteen grandchildren and by the time this is published, fifteen great grandchildren. One of our great joys is the privilege of time spent with them. To two of my beloved friends and brothers in Christ, DeWayne Thomas and Ray Rayburn, both of whom have dedicated their lives to teaching God's word, I thank you. Both are astute Bible scholars who influenced my life more than they will ever know. To Bradley Cobb who graciously helped in preparing this for publication. Finally, to all who will take the time to pick up this writing and apply it to their life, I trust that you will be richly blessed.

Preface

'Believest thou this' are the words of the Savior as He was speaking to Martha, sister of Lazarus, prior to his calling Lazarus forth from the tomb where he had lain for four days.

Jesus was in Jerusalem when He received word that his beloved friend Lazarus was ill. Jesus delayed his departure for two days before going to Bethany, a distance of approximately a mile and a half. He knew that Lazarus was already dead, but He also knew He would resurrect Lazarus from death and the grave.[1] Then said Martha unto Jesus, 'Lord, if thou hadst been here, my brother had not died. But

---

[1] This account is found in the eleventh chapter of the Gospel of John. The quotations made from this chapter are from the King James Version.

I know, that even now, whatsoever thou wilt ask of God, God will give it thee.' Jesus said to Martha, 'Thy brother shall rise again.' It is apparent that Martha understood and had faith in the resurrection at end times. She said to Jesus, 'I know that he shall rise again in the resurrection at the last day,' but evidently lacked understanding of what Jesus intended to do at this time. However, He used this as opportunity to teach another lesson. He said, 'I am the resurrection, and the life: he that believeth in me, though he were dead, yet shall he live: and whosoever liveth and believeth in me shall never die, Believest thou this?' After Jesus had prayed to his Father, He called, 'Lazarus, come forth' and He that was dead came forth. This is *one incident signifying the power that God gave to Jesus during his earthly ministry.* In the words of John, from the last verse in his gospel: 'and there are also many other things which Jesus did, the which, if they should be written every one, I suppose that even the world itself could not contain the books that should be written.' For the purpose of our thoughts now, we will concentrate on the profound and penetrating question that Jesus asked of Martha: *'Believest thou this?'*

'Do you believe' is the way most versions now state the question of Jesus. Whichever way we read it and think on it doesn't change the intent of the piercing question. When we are reading, studying and contemplating the words of the text and realize the vast and percipient truths that are set forth for our enlightenment, do we even come close to discerning what God has chosen to reveal to his creation? Do we truly, without equivocation, *believe*? The Greek word translated *believe* is *'pisteou,'* which denotes far more than simple recognition. I look out my window and see a tree in the front yard. I believe it is a tree. That is recognition. I

look across the street, and I see a house and a car in the driveway. I believe it is a house with a car in the driveway. That is recognition. The Greek word used in the text means far more than recognition. Its intent is to express a grasping onto, a reliance on, to place confidence in and to be obedient to. It is with this thought in mind that we will pursue some issues with which we should be vitally concerned. The question is: *'Believest thou this?'* Do we truly believe and comprehend the teaching of our living God and Father, Creator of all that exists? God granted to man neither the right nor the wisdom to judge any person in any way. Therefore the intent of this book is not to be judgmental but to, hopefully, instill within the reader a desire to read, study, think and meditate deeply on the truths of God's words as revealed to us and what they mean to us.

Chapter One

Do you believe? The first ten words in the Bible are: 'In the beginning God created the heavens and the earth.' Let's stop at that point for now and consider these words. This statement brings to the surface three critical thoughts to consider, two of which are obvious: God and creation. The third is not expressed by word but alluded to by content, and that is the fact of eternity. With a great deal of difficulty, man tries to grasp the meaning of eternity. The finite can never fully comprehend the infinite. Let us deal first with this premise. For anything to make sense and be believed beyond this point, one must embrace the fact of eternity. Eternity is best described as that which has no beginning or end, which always has been and always will be. Failure to acknowledge and believe the fact of eternity is to render meaningless any reason for further study of the

Scriptures. If one cannot accept the truth of eternity, then one cannot accept the existence of an eternal being. To deny eternity is to deny God and to deny his creation. If eternity does not exist then neither does God exist. The three cannot be separated. God, the eternal being IS, always has been, always will be. 'Lord, thou hast been our dwelling-place in all generations. Before the mountains were brought forth, or ever thou hadst formed the earth and the world, even from everlasting to everlasting thou art God.'[1] 'But the Lord is the true God, He is the living God and an everlasting King.'[2] 'He hath made the earth by his power, He hath established the world by his wisdom, and hath stretched out the heavens by his discretion.'[3] 'Thou, even thou, art Lord alone: thou hast made heaven, the heaven of heavens, with all their host, the earth, and all things that are therein, the seas, and all that is therein, and thou preservest them all.'[4] In the beginning, as Moses states in Genesis 1:1, indicates the point at which God decided to create the heavens and the earth.

Prior to creation, the earth was without form and void. It didn't exist. Darkness was upon the face of the deep, and the spirit of God moved upon the face of the waters.[5] From all things non-existent, God began to bring into being all that we witness today. In the process of creation, He made man and woman and set in motion his end purpose: that man could dwell forever in his presence. 'Eternal life, which God, that cannot lie, promised before the world be-

---

[1] Psalm 90:1-2, KJV
[2] Jeremiah 10:10, KJV
[3] Jeremiah 10:12, KJV
[4] Nehemiah 9:6, KJV
[5] Genesis 1:2, KJV

gan.'[1] 'And as Moses lifted up the serpent in the wilderness, even so must the Son of man be lifted up. That whosoever believeth in him should not perish, but have eternal life. For God so loved the world, that he gave his only begotten Son, that whosoever believeth in him should not perish, but have everlasting life. These words were spoken by Jesus Christ. [2]

We have dealt now with eternity. It either exists, or it does not. We have discussed the existence of an eternal being: the omnipotent Creator of all that exists, the all-knowing, all-encompassing, ever present Almighty God. The one true and living God that has revealed Himself through what we see in the natural world, through his Son Jesus Christ and through the Bible. *Do we believe?* Sadly, many do not believe; fortunately, there are multitudes that do believe. How then is it possible for us to accept and believe in matters such as God, eternity, creation, everlasting life and God's revealed word? We cannot see God; we can't reach out and touch Him physically. Did Jesus really come down from heaven and dwell on this earth? We weren't there. We cannot literally open a door and peer into heaven. Does it exist? Are these concepts so nebulous that we are unable to grasp the truths of their existence? These truths are impalpable only if we refuse to accept them through faith.

So then *faith* is the key. Faith is the eye through which we see God and embrace Him for all that He is and all that He does. Then comes the question: how do we acquire faith? The answer: faith can only come through a knowledge of God's word as found in the Bible. 'So then faith cometh by

---

[1] Titus 1:2, KJV
[2] John 3:14-16, KJV

hearing, and hearing by the word of God.'[1] The words of the Bible are God-breathed. 'All Scripture is given by inspiration of God, and is profitable for doctrine, for reproof, for correction, for instruction in righteousness.'[2] Now with those thoughts in mind, let's deal with two more subjects: the Bible and creation.

---

[1] These are the words of the Apostle Paul to the church at Rome, Romans 10:17, KJV

[2] 2nd Timothy 3:16, KJV

Chapter Two

The Bible. The word comes from the Greek word *biblos,* meaning *book*. The Bible is God's book. It is the written record of all that He has revealed for man to know and follow. The Bible is inspired by God, as noted earlier.[1] The Bible is a history of God's dealing with man from man's creation to the present time and beyond to the end time. It is the chronicler of all that is still to come. The Bible is the most unique book ever written. It is the most popular book ever published. It is estimated that more than a hundred million copies of the Bible are sold each year. Divided into the Old Testament and the New Testament, it contains sixty six books and/or letters. Over fifteen centuries in the making and written by more than forty different writers that

---

[1] 2nd Timothy 3:16

were guided by the inspiration of God. Men from all walks of life: prophets, kings and priests, a tax collector, fishermen, a tent maker and a physician. A more diverse group of men would be hard to find. How could this be if it were not controlled by the omniscient God? The Bible is infallible. In its entirety there are no discrepancies. The Old Testament chronicles the coming of a Messiah; the New Testament reveals the fulfillment of God's desires for man: salvation through Christ and his church. As previously stated, the Bible is inerrant. We must then accept it as God's truth, and this we do by faith.

There is an imaginary bridge that closes the gap between what we can see and touch and that which we cannot. That bridge is faith. The writer of the Hebrew letter states: 'Now faith is the substance of things hoped for, the evidence of things not seen…Through faith we understand that the worlds were framed by the word of God, so that things which are seen were not made of things which do appear.'[1] 'Therefore being justified by faith, we have peace with God through our Lord Jesus Christ: by whom also we have access by faith into this grace wherein we stand, and rejoice in hope of the glory of God.'[2] 'These things have I written unto you that believe on the name of the Son of God; that ye may know that ye have eternal life, and that ye may believe on the name of the Son of God.'[3] 'For we walk by faith, not by sight.'[4] 'But without faith it is impossible to please Him: for he that cometh to God must believe that He is, and that He is a rewarder of them that diligently seek

---

[1] Hebrews 11:1, 3, KJV
[2] Romans 5:1-2, KJV
[3] 1 John 5:13, KJV
[4] 2 Corinthians 5:7, KJV

Him.'[1] Is there more that can be stated? Either we believe, or we can choose not to believe. Therefore, let us move on to the final issue we covered as we began our writing. That is the fact of God's creation of all that exists.

---

[1] Hebrews 11:6, KJV

Chapter Three

Is God the creator of all that exists today? That is the question we will deal with at this point. This portion of the writing will require little discussion. Brilliant minds from the scientific community as well as the religious world have set forth differing theories and beliefs for many years. These ideas, beliefs and theories have been debated for centuries without producing a firm conviction that is universally accepted. That being said, it would be counterproductive to spend time going into detail of these various beliefs. For the sake of brevity, let us say as a general rule we are a believer in God and his creation, or we are of the group that believes in one of the various concepts of evolution. We have the right to choose.

At one point in time, a greater percentage of people believed in God and his creation. That is no longer true.

According to a recent Gallup poll, only about four in ten Americans now accept that God is eternal and is the creator of the universe. There are those who wish to accept God but do not believe He is the eternal creator. Some of to-day's religious groups now contend that the idea of evolution does not interfere with their faith in God—a premise hard to reconcile. Again, that is the right of every individual to so believe. We could say it is a God-given right, but that would only add to the debate.

To those who believe in God, it is difficult to comprehend how one would not believe. 'Come and see what God has done, how awesome his works in man's behalf.'[1] 'When I consider your heavens, the work of your fingers, the moon and the stars, which you have set in place.'[2] How can we look at the beauty of the universe and not see God? 'The heavens declare the glory of God; the skies proclaim the works of his hands.'[3] Abraham Lincoln once stated; "I can see how it might be possible for a man to look down upon the earth and be an atheist, but I cannot conceive how he could look up into the heavens and say there is no God." 'By the word of the Lord were the heavens made, their star-ry host by the breath of his mouth.'[4]

Neither with the human eye nor through the instruments of today's technology can we fathom the vastness of the Milky Way that stretches beyond eye or imagination. It is estimated there are at least three hundred fifty billion galax-ies according to Astronomers. This is far beyond man's ability to comprehend. How long has this been in the mak-

[1] Psalm 66:5, NIV
[2] Psalm 8:3, NIV
[3] Psalm 19:1, NIV
[4] Psalm 33:6, NIV

ing? Was there truly some sort of a big bang? There is no definitive answer. We do not know nor do we need to know how God accomplished creation; He did it. Can we look into the heavens and not wonder? How could planet earth be suspended in the midst of the universe? How is it possible that it rotates on its axis at a constant 23.4 degrees away from perpendicular that brings about the seasonal changes? How is it that earth revolves on its axis every twenty-four hours giving us day and night? How does earth, with mechanical precision, orbit the sun once each year? GOD MADE IT SO. 'By faith we understand that the entire universe was formed at God's command, that what we now see did not come from anything that can be seen.'[1] For anything to exist there must be a cause. That cause must have greater power than that which is made to exist. Nothing can come from nothing. There is only one logical determination. Everything that exists is by the all-powerful, eternal God.

---

[1] Hebrews 11:3, NLT

Chapter Four

Having thus considered eternity, God, the eternal being, the Bible and creation, let us continue now with the questioning of ourselves. *'Believest thou this?'* Do we truly believe?

About the year 7 BC, there was a son born to an elderly priest and his wife, Zacharias and Elisabeth. His name was John. His father told him: 'and you, my child, will be called a prophet of the Most High; for you will go on before the Lord to prepare the way for Him.'[1] This John, later to be known as John the baptist, grew up in the wilderness of Judea. When he received the spirit of prophecy, he began to preach there in Judea. Many came to hear him and repented and were baptized in the Jordon River. His message: 're-

---

[1] Luke 1:76, NIV

pent ye: for the kingdom of heaven is at hand.'[1] 'There was a man sent from God, whose name was John. The same came for a witness, to bear witness of the Light that all men through him might believe.'[2] his message was concerning the coming of the Christ, the prophesied Messiah. 'I will raise up a prophet like you from among their fellow Israelites. I will put my words in his mouth, and he will tell the people everything I command him.'[3] As more and more people were hearing of and going to John, priests and Levites were sent from Jerusalem to question him. "Who are you?" they asked him. John replied in the words of Isaiah the prophet. 'I am the voice of one calling in the wilderness. Make straight the way for the Lord.'[4] John told them that one would come after him, the thongs of whose sandals he was not worthy to untie. He was speaking of Jesus. 'The next day John saw Jesus coming toward him and said, Look, the Lamb of God, who takes away the sins of the world! This is the one I meant when I said, A man who comes after me has surpassed me because he was before me. I myself did not know him, but the reason I came baptizing with water was that he might be revealed to Israel.'[5]

The Virgin Mary was to bring forth a child of the Holy Spirit. 'And she shall bring forth a son, and thou shalt call his name Jesus: for he shall save his people from their sins.'[6] 'For God sent not his Son into the world to condemn the world; but that the world through Him might be

---

[1] Matthew 3:2, KJV
[2] John 2:6-7, KJV
[3] Deuteronomy 18:18, NLT
[4] John 1:23, NIV
[5] John 1:29-31, NIV
[6] Matthew 1:32, KJV

saved.'[1] God created man, Adam, and then his wife, Eve. He placed them in the beautiful Garden of Eden where there was everything necessary for life. Their responsibility was to tend and watch over the place that God had given them. God placed only one restriction on them: 'You may freely eat of every tree in the garden except the tree of the knowledge of good and evil.'[2] Being tempted by Satan, they ate the fruit of that tree, and because of their disobedience, they were banished from the garden. Recorded in the third chapter of Genesis, we find the first indication of a coming Savior. 'And I will cause hostility between you and the woman, and between your offspring and her offspring. He will strike your head and you will strike his heel.'[3] Satan was to be the nemesis to Christ and man, but Christ would be the ultimate victor over Satan and sin.

Because of the failure by Adam and Eve to heed God's direction, sin was brought into the world. 'When Adam sinned, sin entered into the world. Adam's sin brought death, so death spread to everyone, for everyone sinned.'[4] Before that sin, man had a close and personal relationship with God. Because of sin, man was now separated from God, and a way to come back to God would be necessary. That is the role the Savior Jesus Christ came to fulfill. It would cost Him his life to do this, but He did it willingly. The Apostle Peter, speaking before the council in Jerusalem, stated: 'There is salvation in no one else. God has given no other name under heaven by which we must be

---

[1] John 3:17, KJV
[2] Genesis 1:16-17, NLT
[3] Genesis 3:15, NLT
[4] Romans 5:12, NLT

saved.'[1] Jesus said; 'I am the way, the truth, and the life: no man cometh to the Father but by me.'[2]

So, we find a loving God who created man in his own image. God who provided for man a place of dwelling that contained all the necessities of life. Man, whom God had made and blessed with the beautiful abode, sinned and because of this, man is estranged from God. There must be a way to be reconciled with God. Christ came to make that reconciliation possible.

---

[1] Acts 3:12, NLT
[2] John 14:6, KJV

Chapter Five

'In the beginning was the Word, and the Word was with God, and the Word was God. He was with God in the beginning. Through him all things were made: without him nothing was made that has been made.'[1] John's words are concerning the Christ who gave up his glorious place in heaven and came to this world to do his Father's bidding, giving his life as a sacrifice for the sins of mankind. In the same chapter, we read: 'The Word became flesh and made his dwelling among us. We have seen his glory, the glory of the One and only, who came from the Father full of grace and truth.'[2] 'For unto you is born this day in the city

---

[1] John 1:1-2, NIV
[2] John 1:14, NIV

of David a Savior, which is Christ the Lord.'[1] This is the Jesus that was conceived by the Holy Spirit; his was a supernatural conception and birth. Not the son of a human father but born as the Son of God. The use of 'Word' (Greek *Logos*) here is clearly referring to Jesus. Jesus was with God, Jesus was God and by Him all things were created. This Jesus lived in the presence of God; He existed before his miraculous conception and birth of the Virgin Mary. 'Behold, a virgin shall be with child, and shall bring forth a son, and they shall call his name Emmanuel, which being interpreted is, God with us.'[2] He was the active agent through whom God created all things.

Jesus, the Son of God, left the presence of God, came to earth by way of a miraculous birth to give his life for the sins of man. To what purpose? He was to be, and is, our propitiation, our atonement for our sins through faith in his blood. 'Yet God, with undeserved kindness, declares that we are righteous. He did this through Christ Jesus when He freed us from the penalty for our sins. For God presented Jesus as the sacrifice for sin. People are made right with God when they believe that Jesus sacrificed his life, shedding his blood.'[3]

Man was estranged from God. Only by God's love could a way be provided for man's reconciliation with Him. John spoke of the extent of this love. 'This is love: not that we loved God, but that he loved us and sent his Son as an atoning sacrifice for our sins.'[4] Jesus Himself said: 'For the Son

---

[1] Luke 2:11, KJV
[2] Matthew 1:23, KJV
[3] Romans 3:24-25, NLT
[4] 1 John 4:10, NIV

of Man came to seek and save what was lost.'[1] From the sin of Adam to the sacrifice of Christ, there was no forgiveness for sin. The ceremonial sacrifices of the Old Testament did not cleanse sin. 'But those sacrifices are an annual reminder of sins, because it is impossible for the blood of bulls and goats to take away sins.'[2] Without the cleansing from sin by the blood of Christ, man would be eternally separated from God.

We must remember that life does not end when we pass beyond the vale of this physical life here on earth. Life goes on, and eternity is never ending. There are those who expound the doctrine of materialism: that all there is to life is that in which we participate while in this physical body. This is to deny God as an eternal being and discount the Bible teaching of eternal life. This being true, it would deny the reason for Jesus giving his life for man to be able to live with God. The Apostle Paul stated in his letter to the Corinthians: 'And if our hope in Christ is only for this life, we are more to be pitied than anyone in the world.'[3]

If there is no life after physical death, then what reason is there for hope and faith? However, we do know from God's word this is not the case. Jesus said: 'I tell you the truth, whoever hears my word and believes him who sent me has eternal life and will not be condemned; he has crossed over from death to life.'[4] 'I write these things to you who believe in the name of the Son of God so that you may know that you have eternal life.'[5] The writer of the

---

[1] Luke 19:10, NIV
[2] Hebrews 10:3-4, NIV
[3] 1 Corinthians 16:19, NLT
[4] John 5:24, NIV
[5] 1 John 5:13, NIV

Hebrew letter tells us: 'Just as man is destined to die once, and after that to face judgment.'[1] Solomon tells us 'after death this physical body will return to the earth; and the spirit will return to God who gave it.'[2] The only hope man has in being reconciled to God and having eternal life in heaven is through Jesus Christ.

We must believe in Jesus as the Son of God; we must be obedient to his will or forever be estranged from God and be eternally lost. God does not want us to be lost; He sent his Son that the world might be reconciled to Him. Jesus told his disciples: 'Go ye into all the world and preach the gospel to every creature. He that believeth and is baptized shall be saved; but he that believeth not shall be damned.'[3] God does not want anyone to perish but desires for all to come to repentance and be obedient to his teaching.[4] 'And it is impossible to please God without faith. Anyone who wants to come to Him must believe that God exists and that He rewards those who sincerely seek Him.'[5] Death of our physical body is certain, and eternity is forever.

Chapter Six

After the Astronauts had landed on the moon, the late President Richard Nixon said: "The greatest moment in human history is when man walked on the moon." Billy Graham's answer to this was: "No, the greatest moment in history was not when man walked on the moon but when God walked on earth." God did this. He was made manifest in the person of Jesus Christ. God had a purpose in Christ's coming to earth, and it was not just some random happenstance. Jesus came to earth to live among man, to perform the miracles He did, to teach the things He taught, to die in the manner in which He did to fulfill the master plan of the Creator, Almighty God.

The message of John the baptist was: 'repent, for the kingdom of God is at hand.' When he saw Jesus he said: 'behold the lamb of God who takes away the sins of the world.' The blood sacrifices under the old law could not remove sin. There had to be a means of reconciling man to God. This was to be accomplished through the life and death of Jesus Christ. Jesus came to earth to do what could be done in no other way. He would give his life in the most sadistic inhumane manner that the Romans could fathom: crucifixion. This Jesus who made the blind to see, the lame to walk, who raised the dead and healed the sick would give his life for the sins of mankind. When it was time for Him to fulfill God's plan, the Chief Priests and Elders of the Jews bore false witness against Him. They accused Him of blasphemy against God and cried out for his death.

After the Governor, Pontius Pilate, had scourged Jesus, he released Him to the Roman soldiers. They spit on Him, hit Him on the head with reeds, plaited a crown of thorns to place on his head and mocked Him. Jesus was forced to bear the cross upon which He was to be crucified. Outside the walls of Jerusalem to a hill called Golgotha (place of the skull) Jesus was placed on the cross and his wrists and ankles were nailed to the cross. Jesus took upon Himself the sins of all mankind, shed his blood and endured the cruel death in order that man could be reconciled to God. 'For if, when we were enemies, we were reconciled to God by the death of his Son, much more, being reconciled, we shall be saved by his life.'[1] 'But now in Christ Jesus you who once were far away have been brought near through the blood of Jesus Christ.'[2] The Apostle Paul was assuring all men of every nation that through the blood of Christ reconciliation would be possible. 'In Him we have redemption through his blood, the forgiveness of sins, in

---

[1] Romans 5:10, KJV
[2] Ephesians 2:13, NIV

accordance with the riches of God's grace.'[1] 'For He has rescued us from the dominion of darkness and brought us into the kingdom of the Son He loves, in whom we have redemption, the forgiveness of sins.'[2] The kingdom of the Son. Mankind's only means of escape from sin. This is not a worldly physical kingdom, but his spiritual kingdom on earth—his body, his church.

The word *church* means the 'called out': 'church' does not mean a building, a structure made of brick and mortar, a frame work with a sign on the front. *Church* is a divine entity created by the will of God. This is the kingdom purchased with the blood of Christ, and entrance into this kingdom will be through the blood of Christ. Jesus said: 'I will build my church (kingdom) and the gates of hell shall not prevail against it.'[3] The kingdom is built upon the fact that Jesus Christ is the Son of God, the true foundation of this kingdom, his church.

It is appropriate at this time to point out the fact that the church does not have a name, simply 'the church.' It is recognized by the name of its owner. God's church, church of God, Christ's church, church of Christ, church of the Firstborn which is Jesus Christ, the Father's church, God's house, church of the living God, etc., none of which give the church a name, but simply shows to whom the church belongs. Prophesies of old spoke of the coming of the church. 'And it shall come to pass in the latter days that the mountain of Jehovah's house shall be established on the top of the mountains, and shall be exalted above the hills; and all nations shall flow unto it. And many peoples shall go

---

[1] Ephesians 1:7, NIV
[2] Colossians 1:13-14, NIV
[3] Matthew 16:18, KJV

and say, Come ye, and let us go up to the mountain of Jehovah, to the house of the God of Jacob; and he will teach us his ways, and we shall walk in his paths: for out of Zion shall go forth the law, and word of Jehovah from Jerusalem.'[1] God speaking through the prophet Isaiah indicated the coming of the kingdom and the location of its establishment, and that it would be exalted above everything. Let us continue to question ourselves as we go into the next pertinent thoughts.

---

[1] Isaiah 2:2-3, KJV

Chapter Seven

As stated in the preface of this writing, there is no intent whatsoever to be judgmental in this effort. We will continue our study of the kingdom of Christ, his church, and nothing will be considered other than those truths we garner from a reading and study of the Bible. We rely totally on the teachings which are found in God's word. It is sufficient to satisfy all questions and concerns. 'All Scripture is inspired by God and is useful to teach us what is true and to make us realize what is wrong in our lives. It corrects us when we are wrong and teaches us to do what is right. God uses it to prepare and equip his people to do every good work.'[1] 'Above all, you must realize that no prophecy in Scripture ever came from the prophet's own understanding,

---

[1] 2 Timothy 3:16-17, NLT

or from human initiative. No, those prophets were moved by the Holy Spirit, and they spoke from God.'[1] Jesus instructed the Apostles to go preach, saying the kingdom of heaven is at hand.[2] He said: 'I tell you the truth, some standing here right now will not die before they see the Kingdom of God arrive in great power.'[3] From these Scriptures we can safely conclude that the time for the establishment of Christ's kingdom, his church, was in the offing.

As we turn to the book of Acts, we find the fulfillment of the prophecies and Christ's teaching. In the first chapter of Acts, we read of Jesus giving instruction to the chosen Apostles. Christ was crucified at the time of the Passover feast; He was in the tomb for three days and then resurrected and presented Himself several times to the disciples. 'During the forty days after his resurrection, He appeared to the apostles from time to time, and he proved to them in many ways that he was actually alive. And He talked to them about the Kingdom of God.'[4] Jesus further instructed them: 'Do not leave Jerusalem until the Father sends you the gift He promised, as I told you before, John baptized with water, but in just a few days you will be baptized with the Holy Spirit.'[5] 'You will receive power when the Holy Spirit comes upon you. And you will be my witnesses, telling people about me everywhere, in Jerusalem, throughout Judea, in Samaria and to the ends of the earth.'[6] As Jesus was completing these instructions He was taken up into a

---

[1] 2 Peter 1:20-21, NLT
[2] Matthew 10:7, KJV
[3] Mark 9:1, NLT
[4] Acts 1:3, NLT
[5] Acts 1:4-5, NLT
[6] Acts 1:8, NLT

cloud while they were watching. He was returned to Heaven as was prophesied and as He stated. 'After the Lord Jesus had spoken to them, he was taken up into heaven and He sat at the right hand of God.'[1] 'But from now on, the Son of Man will be seated at the right hand of the mighty God.'[2]

From these Scriptures we know that Jesus, having completed his earthly ministry, returned to heaven. He had taught his disciples, He had healed the sick, made the lame to walk, caused the blind to see and prepared the Apostles for their mission. Then, He willingly gave his life as the supreme sacrifice for the sins of mankind. His final words as life ebbed from his body, "it is finished." With that, He bowed his head and gave up his spirit.[3] Jesus wasn't saying his life was finished. He had completed his mission here on earth, all prophesies were now fulfilled and the price for sin was paid. He had finished all that He came to earth to do.

[1] Mark 16:19, NIV
[2] Luke 22:69, NIV
[3] John 19:30, NIV

Chapter Eight

After receiving instructions from Jesus to wait for the gift of the Holy Spirit and witnessing Jesus being caught up in the cloud, the Apostles went back into Jerusalem. It was during this interim that Peter reminded those gathered that they needed to find a replacement for Judas who had betrayed Christ. It would require one who had been with Jesus from the time of his baptism until his ascension. Two men were nominated, Barsabbas (also known as Justus) and Matthias. Then they prayed to God for guidance, and after the prayers, they cast lots and Matthias was chosen to be numbered among the Apostles.[1]

On the day of Pentecost (the first Pentecost following the ascension of Christ) we are told the disciples were gathered

---

[1] These events are recorded in Acts chapter one.

in one place. 'Suddenly there was a sound from heaven like the roaring of a mighty windstorm, and it filled the house where they were sitting. Then what looked like flames or tongues of fire appeared and settled on each of them. And everyone present was filled with the Holy Spirit and began speaking in other languages as the Holy Spirit gave them this ability.'[1]

The feast of Pentecost came fifty days after the Passover. Most historians considered it the greatest Jewish feast of the year. The Jews were scattered over the Roman Empire. It is very likely there were more Jews in Jerusalem on Pentecost than at any other time. We are told that devout Jews from every nation were present at this time.[2] There were fifteen countries named and likely a dozen or more dialects spoken, yet each heard the Apostles speaking in their native language. It should be noted here that the Holy Spirit came only to those Apostles, not all of the one hundred twenty in the room. In verse seven of the second chapter of Acts it is stated: 'these people are all from Galilee.' Not all that were in the room were from Galilee. The Scriptures do not tell us how it came to be that all the people began to gather. It could have been the sound that seemed to be a roaring wind; it is possible it is because of the Apostles speaking in different languages, possibly for both reasons. As the Apostles were speaking, the people gathered to hear them. They stood there 'amazed and perplexed. What can this mean?' they asked each other. Some in the crowd even accused them of being drunk.

'Then Peter stepped forward with the eleven other Apostles and shouted to the crowd, Listen carefully, all of you fellow

---

[1] Acts 2:2-4, NLT
[2] Acts 2:5

Jews and residents of Jerusalem! Make no mistake about this, these people are not drunk, as some of you are assuming. Nine o'clock in the morning is much too early for that. No, what you see was predicted long ago by the prophet.'[1] Then Peter quoted to them the words of God as recorded in the book of Joel[2] concerning the coming of a Savior and a look into the final dispensation of time. The Christian era, the revealing of the plan that God had for the redemption of man, the beginning of the church would all begin on this notable day.

As Peter spoke to them, he reminded them of truths they would know, or *should* know from the prophecies that foretold the events taking place. The last days had come and God had poured forth his Spirit to empower the Apostles to teach. Peter had been appointed spokesman; he had been given the 'keys of the kingdom.' They had looked for the coming Messiah and the Messiah had come, but they rejected Him. The Messiah, the Son of God, proved among them by the miracles, which Peter called 'mighty works and wonders and signs which God did by Him in the midst of you.' He reminded them that Jesus was delivered to the Roman authorities by the Jews, and that Jesus was crucified, but that God had raised Him from the dead and had taken Him back into heaven to be seated at the right hand of God. Peter continues, 'Therefore let all Israel be assured of this: God has made this Jesus, whom you crucified, both Lord and Christ. When the people heard this they were cut to the heart and said to Peter and the other Apostles, Brothers what shall we do? Peter replied, 'Repent and be baptized every one of you, in the name of Jesus Christ for

[1] Acts 2:14-16, NLT
[2] Joel 2:28-32

the forgiveness of your sins. And you will receive the gift of the Holy Spirit. The promise is for you and your children and for all who are far off—for all whom the Lord our God will call. With many other words he warned them; and he pleaded with them, save yourselves from this corrupt generation. Those who accepted his message were baptized and about three thousand were added to their number that day.'[1] At this exact time, as those new believers repented and were baptized into Christ, his church had its beginning. Without question this was the most momentous event ever in recorded history. The only kingdom wherein man can be reconciled with God was brought into existence! God's plan to provide man a means of salvation came to fruition! We are not privy to the entirety of Peters preaching at that time. We do know he spoke many other words, however, what he spoke convinced many of their errors and estrangement from God. We were told the kingdom would come with power.[2] That power was the Holy Spirt,[3] and it was through the Holy Spirt that Peter and the other Apostles were able to speak in the several dialects of those present.

On this Pentecost day the church came into existence as individuals were baptized into Christ. From that day, nearly two thousand years ago, to the present, what made members of the church then still makes members of the church today. There are no other instructions from God's word; nothing is different today than it was on that day. Individuals turned from their old beliefs, believed that Jesus is the Son of God and were baptized into Christ for the remission of sins. These truths were established at that time and have

---

[1] Acts 2:36-41, NIV
[2] Mark 9:1, KJV
[3] Acts 1:8

not changed in any way, shape, or form since. When people believe that Jesus is the Christ, the Son of God, repent and turn away from the past life, confesses their belief and are baptized, they are cleansed of sin and are added to the church that belongs to Christ. Jesus said: 'I am the way, the truth, and the life. No one can come to the Father except through me.'[1] 'Salvation is found in no one else, for there is no other name under heaven given to men by which we must be saved.'[2] True when the statements were made, true today.

The requirements to become a Christian, to belong to the church that was established on the aforementioned Pentecost, are simple and easily understood. It is quite unfortunate that in the ensuing years man has chosen to depart from the simple teaching of our Lord. This is not to precipitate nor to perpetuate any sort of debate or to discuss ongoing differences that man has created through the years since the church had its beginning. There is nothing to debate, either we believe God's word or we don't. We see hundreds of differing doctrines offered in today's world of religious practices. Is this satisfactory with God? To answer that question is not the office of the writer. The answer lies in a diligent search of what God has set forth.[3] Search the Scriptures, and then form your own answer. Like the people of Berea, we should search the Scriptures daily to learn the truth.[4]

We will leave this at this point for each individual to contemplate with a couple of final thoughts. 'But even if we or

---

[1] John 14:6, NLT
[2] Acts 4:12, NIV
[3] 2 Timothy 2:15
[4] Acts 17:11

an angel from heaven should preach a gospel other than the one we preached to you, let him be eternally condemned! As we have already said, so now I say again: if anybody is preaching to you a gospel other than what you accepted, let him be eternally condemned.'[1] 'And I solemnly declare to everyone who hears the words of prophecy written in this book: If anyone adds anything to what is written here, God will add to that person the plagues described in this book. And if anyone removes any of the words from this book of prophecy, God will remove that person's share in the tree of life and in the holy city that are described in this book.'[2] Do we believe?

---

[1] Galatians 1:8-9, NIV
[2] Revelation 22:18-19, NLT

Chapter Nine

We have now witnessed, through the eyes of God's teaching, the establishment of the promised kingdom of the Lord Jesus Christ. Old Testament prophesies foretold the coming of this kingdom. Jesus spoke of the coming of his kingdom. After his death, burial, and resurrection, He further taught his disciples of the coming kingdom. On the Pentecost after his ascension into heaven, the Holy Spirit came upon the Apostles, and as they taught, people believed and were baptized into Christ, added to his body which is his church. Now, in view of all we have discussed to this point, we might ask the question: *for what purpose does the kingdom exist?* Death and the destiny of man beyond the grave is the reason for the kingdom, the church. In perhaps one of the earliest books in the Bible, Job asked: 'If a man die shall he live again?'[1] There is no question of man's dying. 'And as it is appointed unto to man once to die, but after this the judgment.'[2] 'And the Lord God formed man of the dust of the ground, and breathed into his nostrils the breath of life; and man became a living being.'[3] 'Then the dust will return to the earth as it was, and the spirit will return to God who gave it.'[4] 'Whereas ye know not what shall be on the morrow. For what is your life? It is even a vapor that appeareth for a little time and vanisheth away.'[5]

God formed Adam from the dust of the ground, and the Bible tells us this physical body will return to the ground. Death is inevitable. Whether we live twenty years, sixty years or ninety years, our physical body will die. Unless we should still be alive when Christ returns, the death rate is one hundred percent. Man has many choices in this life; he can make decisions that can change his life or perhaps the lives of many thousands, but he cannot choose *not* to die. But as we can know from the Scriptures above, death is not the end. It is simply a passing from this physical life here on earth to the realm beyond the grave. Life does not end in a box in a church building or a funeral home; it does not end with ashes in an urn. Life simply does not end; it goes on. The word *death* means not an end but a *separation*. When one is conceived in the mother's womb, that embryo enters eternity; eternity is forever. When we come to an understanding of this fact, the reason for an eternal kingdom becomes evident and most important. Life beyond this physical plane is assured by God's promises.

---

[1] Job 14:14, NIV
[2] Hebrews 9:27, KJV
[3] Genesis 2:7, NKJV
[4] Ecclesiastes 12:7, NKJV
[5] James 4:14, KJV

The Hebrew writer tells us it is appointed unto man once to die and then the judgment. Now, we understand that not only will we experience physical death, but that there will be a judgment. What does this mean? Judgment is a decision made by one empowered to render impartial judgment between two or more factors. Following the decision of the judge, there will be a ruling. The judgment of which the writer of Hebrews speaks is the divine judgment by Jesus Christ that will determine our eternal dwelling place after we are separated from this physical life on earth. Peter, speaking to the household of Cornelius says: 'He (Jesus) commanded us to preach to the people and to testify that He is the one whom God appointed as judge of the living and the dead.'[1] 'Marvel not at this: for the hour is coming in the which all that are in the graves shall hear his voice, and shall come forth; they that have done good unto the resurrection of life, and they that have done evil unto the resurrection of damnation.'[2] That will be the time of judgment and the ruling that follows. 'For we must all stand before Christ to be judged. We will each receive whatever we deserve for the good or evil we have done in this earthly body.'[3] We can be assured of fair and impartial judgment by Christ. 'But if you do what is wrong, you will be paid back for the wrong you have done. For God has no favorites.'[4]

So, we accept the reality of death. We understand from God's word the spirit of man will live beyond the passing of the earthly body. It is apparent that each of us will appear before Christ at some point and face judgment for

---

[1] Acts 10:32, NIV
[2] John 5:28-29, KJV
[3] 2 Corinthians 5:10, NLT
[4] Colossians 3:25, NLT

what our life has or has not been, for He said each person will enter into either to the resurrection of life or the resurrection of death. Obviously, it is extremely important then to know what will be the determining factors that secure our place in the end of all things. All the above truths from God's Holy Scriptures point us to several unquestionable conclusions.

1. God created man.
2. Man disobeyed God and brought sin into the world.
3. Man needed a means of being reconciled to God.
4. God sent his Son to earth to facilitate a means of reconciliation.
5. The Son gave his life as a sacrifice for man's sins.
6. After the Son was crucified, buried and resurrected, He returned to his heavenly home with his Father, and his spiritual kingdom, his church, his body was established.
7. His kingdom became reality on the Pentecost day following his ascending to heaven.
8. His kingdom came into being with power: the power of the direction of the Holy Spirit.

These conclusions are not based on supposition; they are simply facts stated in God's word. Now, let's tuck these thoughts in the back of our mind for further contemplation and explore a few more thoughts pertinent to our study.

$\mathfrak{Chapter\ Ten}$

The eight unquestionable conclusions as stated above will
need further exploration to be better understood. It should
be stated at this point, as all should realize, we are dealing
with the factors that determine where we will be for eternity. As important as this is, we must then continue to
consider *only* those truths we find in the Bible. We must
not rely on any other source. If our hope is eternal life in
the presence of our God, then we surely can depend on his
words in the Bible for our guidance. 'For whatsoever things
were written aforetime were written for our learning, that
we through patience and comfort of the Scriptures might
have hope.'[1]

---

[1] Romans 15:4, KJV

We have established the fact that man will die; this physical body will eventually cease to exist. Our focus now will deal with what happens after death. We have already determined that the physical body will no longer exist, but that the spirit of man lives on. We know from the Hebrew letter that after death will be, in time, the judgment. That judgment will come when Jesus returns for the purpose of passing his judgment on man. It will be a time of separation; his determination of who shall have everlasting life and who shall be eternally condemned. 'Marvel not at this: for the hour is coming, in the which all that are in the graves shall hear his voice, and shall come forth; they that have done good to the resurrection of life, and they that have done evil, unto the resurrection of damnation.'[1] Jesus said: 'For the Father judgeth no man, but hath committed all judgment unto the Son.'[2] Paul, the Apostle of Jesus, states: "that there shall be a resurrection of the dead, both of the just and the unjust.'[3]

We can know from these Scriptures then that those who will be saved eternally will be separated from those who will be lost eternally at the time of resurrection and judgment. The Apostle Paul tells us: 'for if we have been planted together in the likeness of his death, we shall be also in the likeness of his resurrection.'[4] To the church at Thessalonica, Paul wrote: 'And now, dear brothers and sisters we want you to know what will happen to the believers who have died so you will not grieve like people who have no hope. For since we believe that Jesus died and was raised to life again, we also believe that when Jesus returns God will bring back with Him the believers who

---

[1] John 5:28-29, KJV
[2] Matthew 5:22, KJV
[3] Acts 24:15b, KJV
[4] Romans 6:5, KJV

have died. We tell you this directly from the Lord: We who are still living when the Lord returns will not meet Him ahead of those who have died. For the Lord Himself will come down from heaven with a commanding shout, with the voice of the archangel, and with the trumpet call of God. First, the Christians who have died will rise from their graves. Then together with them, we who are still alive and remain on the earth will be caught up in the clouds to meet the Lord in the air. Then we will be with the Lord forever.'[1] Again, the words of the Apostle Paul: 'Listen, I tell you a mystery: We will not all fall asleep, but we will be changed—in a flash, in the twinkling of an eye, at the last trumpet. For the trumpet will sound, the dead will be raised imperishable and we will be changed. For the perishable must clothe itself with the imperishable, and the mortal with immortality.'[2] Mortal bodies which are perishable will no longer be subject to dying. The dead in Christ and those still on earth will be changed to immortal beings.

Jesus will make the ruling on who will live on in eternal bliss and who will live on in eternal condemnation. Each of us will have to stand before Him for this ruling. 'For we must all appear before the judgment seat of Christ; that every one may receive the things done in his body, according to that he hath done, whether it be good or bad.'[3] 'For it is written, As I live saith the Lord, every knee shall bow to Me and every tongue shall confess to God. So then every one of us shall give account of himself to God.'[4] There is no question that everyone will eventually bow his knee and confess his belief in God. The critical element is *when* we

---

[1] 1 Thessalonians 4:13-17, NLT
[2] 1 Corinthians 15:51-53, NIV
[3] 2 Corinthians 5:10, KJV
[4] Romans 4:11-12, KJV

do it. To be of any benefit to the saving of our soul we must do it while living. If we don't do it while in this life, we will do it on the other side, but it will not change our destination then. We will still be condemned because we did not do it in this life. Jesus said: 'He that rejecteth me and receiveth not my words, hath one that judgeth him; the word that I have spoken, the same shall judge him in the last day.'[1] There can be no doubt in the mind of anyone then that there will come a time of resurrection and judgment.

---

[1] John 12:48, KJV

Chapter Eleven

With these thoughts firmly established in our mind, facts of which there can be no question, let us think further. We must consider what will be the outcome for each of us at this time of judgment. None of the above truths are based on guessing or assumption, nor on the doctrine of any man's thinking that is contrary to that which is taught in God's word. The end result of all of life is that we will either enjoy eternal life in the presence of the Lord or we will suffer eternally in torment with no hope of escape. Jesus said: 'Verily, verily, I say unto you. He that believeth on me hath everlasting life.'[1] Jesus said: 'And this is the will of Him that sent me, that everyone that seeth the Son, and

---

[1] John 6:47, KJV

believeth on Him, may have everlasting life: and I will
raise him up at the last day.'[1]

The word of God tells us there are only two outcomes to
which we can look forward—Eternal life in the place prepared for the believers, and eternal punishment for failing
to acknowledge the Savior. Listen to the comforting words
of Jesus. 'Don't let your hearts be troubled. Trust in God,
and trust also in me. There is more than enough room in my
Father's home. If this were not so, would I have told you
that I am going to prepare a place for you? When everything is ready, I will come and get you, so that you will
always be with me where I am. And you know the way to
where I am going.'[2] Then compare the words of the Apostle Paul writing to the Christians at Thessalonica: 'And God
will provide rest for you who are being persecuted and also
for us when the Lord Jesus appears from heaven. He will
come with his mighty angels in flaming fire, bringing
judgment on those who don't know God and on those who
refuse to obey the Good News of our Lord Jesus. They will
be punished with eternal destruction, forever separated
from the Lord and from his glorious power.'[3] 'Tribulation
and anguish, upon every soul of man that doeth evil, of the
Jew first, and also of the Greek [Gentile].'[4]

Now let us consider these things. We have established from
the unquestionable words of God that physical death is not
the end. We have shown there will be a continuing existence in the realm we understand as eternity: that which has
no beginning and no end, it always was and always will be.

---

[1] John 6:40, KJV
[2] John 14:1-4, NLT
[3] 2 Thessalonians 1:7-9, NLT
[4] Romans 2:9, KJV

In this chapter and previous chapters we have established the fact of a coming judgment and a separation between those who will have eternal bliss and those who will live on in eternal punishment, which will be the second death. These truths being considered then, our choice of eternal bliss or eternal punishment, wherein does our hope lie? 'Because of our faith, Christ has brought us into this place of undeserved privilege where we now stand and we confidently and joyfully look forward to sharing God's glory.'[1] Where is this place of which the Apostle Paul is speaking? According to Scripture, it must be the kingdom of Christ. 'For He has rescued us from the kingdom of darkness and transferred us in to the Kingdom of his dear Son, who purchased our freedom and forgave our sins.'[2] It is abundantly clear that our hope is in Jesus Christ and his Kingdom, the Kingdom of God, the Kingdom of Heaven.

As previously validated, this is not an earthly kingdom as we understand the word *kingdom*, but rather a *spiritual* kingdom established on the aforementioned Pentecost. This spiritual kingdom will exist in this last dispensation of time: that is, until Christ comes again. At that time those in the Kingdom of Christ will be in Christ forever in eternal glory. 'Christ loved the church. He gave up his life for her to make her holy and clean, washed by the cleansing of God's word. He did this to present her to himself as a glorious church without a spot or wrinkle or any other blemish. Instead she will be holy and without fault.'[3] 'Christ is the head of the church. He is the Savior of his body, the church.'[4] 'God has put all things under the au-

---

[1] Romans 5:2, NLT
[2] Colossians 1:13, NLT
[3] Ephesians 5:25b-27, NLT
[4] Ephesians 5:23b, NLT

thority of Christ and has made him head over all things for the benefit of the church. And the church is his body; it is made full and complete by Christ, who fills all things everywhere with himself.'[1] The only logical and scriptural conclusion then, at which we must arrive, is that the kingdom is the body of Christ, his church. Those in this kingdom, the church, will be those who will live forever in the presence of the Savior. Those outside the kingdom will be eternally lost. With these truths established from God's own words, the Holy Scriptures, let us explore further facts about the kingdom and its significance to all mankind.

---

[1] Ephesians 1:22-23, NLT

Chapter Twelve

When we consider the brevity of our time here on earth, we realize that however many years we may enjoy, life lasts but for a very short time. Even if we achieve the three score and ten or by reason of strength we see four score years, they will pass quickly. 'Why, you do not even know what will happen tomorrow. What is your life? You are a mist that appears for a little while and then vanishes.'[1] Whether or not we choose to embrace this truth, it is still the absolute truth. This being fact, how much time do we have allotted to us to make preparation for the end of this life and the life that lies ahead? There is no definitive answer to this question. The only thing we can know without doubt is that life on this earth is, at best, very short.

---

[1] James 4:14, NIV

From our study of the Scriptures, we can conclude that life will continue after this physical body is used up. We also realize there will be a time of reckoning when we will answer to our Lord for what our life has been. One way or another we know that every knee shall bow and every tongue shall confess to God, and we will all give account of ourselves to God. As already stated, it is a fact that we will confess that Jesus is the Christ. We will either embrace this truth while we have the opportunity in this life, or we will do it in the end of time when it will be too late. These truths are unquestionable; we can only conclude then that we must stand in readiness to meet our Lord Jesus Christ. Realizing these truths then should give us pause to consider what *is* and what is *not* truly important.

We are so easily caught up in the pursuits of this world that we are prone to forget the things that are to come and the things of genuine importance. It is so easy to focus on material matters because of the environment in which we live. We are constantly bombarded with suggestions and demands from the media, from our associates, from our family and from our own misdirected thinking that certain goals of achievement are all that matters. Unfortunately, this is not good. It matters not in the end what our worldly gains might be. What is important, and the only thing that can be of any value, is our relationship with God. Can we believe otherwise? We will not be evaluated by the amount of money we have accumulated, by the size of the home in which we live, what kind of prestigious automobile we possess nor the accolades from our fellow man. When all is said and done and the end comes, what will count is whether or not we are in the Kingdom of Christ. These truths being undeniable then in the words of Peter: 'what manner of people should we be?' There is a simple answer for that question.

Let's revisit the words of Jesus: 'For God loved the world so much that he gave his one and only Son, so that everyone who believes in him will not perish but have eternal life.'[1] Jesus told his eleven disciples: 'Go into all the world and preach the Good News to everyone. Anyone who believes and is baptized will be saved. But anyone who refuses to believe will be condemned.'[2] Harsh? Not in the least, just a simple invitation from our Lord to believe in Him and to become a member of his Kingdom. It is just a matter of our choosing our course in life. Peter tells us: 'The Lord isn't really slow about his promise, as some people think. No, he is being patient for your sake. He does not want anyone to be destroyed, but wants everyone to repent.'[3]

Jesus pointed out that his coming was to save the world[4] but that He would save only those who were in Him, his Kingdom, his body the church. Jesus said: 'I am the way, the truth and the life. No one can come to the Father except through me."[5] Jesus also said: 'Not everyone who calls out to me, Lord, Lord will enter the Kingdom of Heaven. Only those who actually do the will of my Father in heaven will enter.'[6] These are the words of the Savior; God wants everyone to come to repentance in order to be saved. To repent is to turn away from our past life, to leave the realm of sin and darkness and come into the light of his kingdom by

---

[1] John 3:16, NLT
[2] Mark 16:15-16, NLT
[3] 2 Peter 3:9, NLT
[4] John 3:17
[5] John 14:6, NLT
[6] Matthew 7:21, NLT

way of obedience to his directions. If God does not want us to be lost and Jesus gave his life, shed his blood that we might be cleansed from sin, how much simpler can it be? When God created man, He made man a creature with a will. Man can determine his course. In view of all the above writing from God's word, which course makes the most sense? But the one important fact remains, *choose* we must. Let's think on these things as we explore more about the Kingdom of Christ.

Chapter Thirteen

When we adhere to the word of God, we can understand, without question, what constitutes the Kingdom of God, the Kingdom of Christ, the body of Christ which is his church. As pointed out previously, the Apostle Paul tells us: 'Christ is the head of the church: and he is the Savior of the body. That He loved the church and gave himself for it and that God gave him to be head over all things to the church, which is his body. And he is the head of the body the church.' These passages of Scripture can be verified in Ephesians chapters 1 and 5, as well as Colossians 1. It must be then, without chance of misunderstanding, when we listen to God's word that we have the knowledge necessary to be saved. It is *believing* the word of God and *accepting* it as truth that we can know we will have eternal life with Him; that we can be in his body, of which He will be the

Savior. Remember that Jesus said there is no other way than through Him. These truths show us the way of salvation and are not the teachings of any other than God Himself. Do we question ourselves at this point? To question the path we are on is a good thing.

When all is said and done, when life is over for us, on which pathway will we be found? Jesus said: 'We can enter God's Kingdom only through the narrow gate. The highway to hell is broad, and its gate is wide for the many who choose that way. But the gateway to life is very narrow and the road is difficult and only a few ever find it.'[1] To be numbered as one of 'the few,' we can only conclude, we must be in Christ. Do we wonder just how many is a few? We have no way of knowing, and as far as each individual is concerned, it really doesn't matter. Our concern should lie in knowing that we are following Christ and none other. By so doing we can know we are one of the few. Could we imagine anything that can give us more comfort than knowing we are in Christ, in his Kingdom, his church?

Let's look again at the words of Paul: 'For whatsoever things were written aforetime were written for our learning, that we through patience and comfort of the Scriptures might have hope.'[2] Paul was speaking of the Scriptures of the Old Testament which served as a guide to understanding the teaching of the New Testament period, ushered in with the establishment of Christ's Kingdom. We gain our hope and thereby our comfort in learning the truths of the Bible. Only by following the word of God will anyone enter into the Kingdom of God. Without any doubt then we

---

[1] Matthew 7:13-14, NLT
[2] Romans 15:4, KJV

should make it our first priority to know how we are to enter into this Kingdom. Doesn't this make sense?

We realize, in the end time, we will be relegated to a realm of eternal bliss or eternal torment. Being aware of these truths, does it not make the decision process simple? Surely it must. Why would any thinking person choose eternal punishment when an eternity in the presence of God and his glorious realm is the alternate choice?

Our question then should be: How do we gain entrance into the Kingdom that will be saved? Remember, Jesus said that no one could come to the Father except through Him. It is simple to conclude then that we must be in Jesus Christ, in his Kingdom, his body the church. John, speaking of Christ, said: 'He came to his own people, and even they rejected Him. But to all who believed him and accepted him, he gave the right to become children of God.'[1] We have already realized that God is not willing that anyone should perish, but that all should repent. Christ, the Son of God, is the author of salvation—but only to them that obey him.[2] So then, the right to become children of God is exercised by believing and obeying the Christ. Paul said: 'Don't you realize that you become the slave of whatever you choose to obey? You can be a slave to sin, which leads to death, or you can choose to obey God, which leads to righteous living.'[3] Again, the choice of which pathway we should choose seems quite simple. If we are to be obedient to Christ in order to be in Him and be saved, we might mimic the question of the people on Pentecost: 'Men and brethren what shall we do?' Peter answered: 'Repent and

---

[1] John 1:11-12, NLT
[2] Hebrews 5:9
[3] Romans 6:16, NLT

be baptized every one of you in the name of Jesus Christ for the remission of your sins, and ye shall receive the gift of the Holy Spirit.'[1]

Since that day to the present day, nothing has changed. What believers did at that time made them members of the body of Christ. People believing today and being baptized makes them members of the body of Christ. By their obedience to the teaching of the Apostles, they were added to the church, the Kingdom of which we have been reading.

In Matthew the sixteenth chapter we read of Peter's answer to Christ's question of who Peter understood Christ to be. Peter said: 'you are the Christ, the Son of the Living God.'[2] To this statement of fact Christ replied: 'Blessed are you, Simon son of Jonah. For this was not revealed to you by man, but by my Father in heaven. And I tell you that you are Peter (Greek *Petros*) and upon this rock (Greek *Petra*) I will build my church and the gates of Hades will not overcome it.'[3] We pause here to distinguish between the two Greek words *Petros* and *Petra* so as not to be confused with the intent of the passage. The name Peter (*Petros*) means here a stone, in the Greek language it is used in the masculine gender. It would refer to the firmness and boldness of the man Peter. The Greek, *Petra*, means a large shelf or ledge of rock and is in the feminine form and refers to the foundation upon which Jesus would build his church. It would not be built on a stone but rather on this large mass of rock which would provide the correct foundation for the church. Meaning it would be built upon the fact that Jesus is indeed the Son of the Living God. 'For other foun-

[1] Acts 2:37-38, KJV
[2] Matthew 16:16, NIV
[3] Matthew 16:17-18, NIV

dation can no man lay than that is laid, which is Jesus Christ.'[1]

Jesus said to Peter: 'I will give you the keys of the Kingdom of heaven; whatever you bind on earth will be bound in heaven, and whatever you loose on earth will be loosed in heaven.'[2] Peter had the authority from Jesus to set the terms for entry into the Kingdom. On the aforementioned day of Pentecost when the Apostles were speaking to the gathered crowd in Jerusalem, Peter, by the direction of the Holy Spirit *did* set out the terms of entry. In that crowd of people there were those convinced that Jesus was the Christ. They wanted to know what they should do. They were instructed to repent and be baptized in the name of Jesus Christ for the remission of sin. 'And the Lord added to the church daily such as should be saved.'[3] There can be no question of when the Kingdom, the church, had its beginning. There can be no doubt about how we enter the church. We have assurance that the Kingdom, the church, will live on in eternity, that Jesus will be the Savior of that body. Can we even begin to imagine a place that we would rather be?

---

[1] 1 Corinthians 3:11, KJV
[2] Matthew 16:19, NIV
[3] Acts 2:47b, KJV

Chapter Fourteen

It has been established by the teaching from God's word that the church is that body which will be saved by the Savior, Jesus Christ. That the church will dwell in God's heavenly realm, time unending. At the risk of being repetitious let's pursue a little further a few thoughts pertinent to our study. Perhaps we should question ourselves a bit more concerning the things we truly embrace. We understand that believers who wish to enter the kingdom do so by repenting and being baptized into Christ. 'Or don't you know that all of us who were baptized into Christ Jesus were baptized into his death? We were therefore buried with him through baptism into death in order that, just as Christ was raised from the dead through the glory of the Father, we too may live a new life.'[1] 'For as many of you as have been baptized into Christ have put on Christ.'[2]

At this point let's have a definite understanding of the meaning of baptism. From Romans 6, previously quoted, baptism is a *burial*. Baptize is the anglicized Greek word *Baptizo,* which means to *immerse*. In being baptized one is complying in a solemn act of obedience to God. Just as Christ was crucified, buried and resurrected, we in like manner die to the old man by repenting, buried in the water by being baptized and rise out of the water a new creature, a new person. 'For if we have been planted together in the likeness of his death, we shall be also in the likeness of his resurrection; knowing this, that our old man is crucified with him, that the body of sin might be destroyed, that henceforth we should not serve sin.'[3] 'Therefore if any man be in Christ, he is a new creature: old things have passed away; behold, all things are become new.'[4] We know, then, when one complies with these tenets they receive the gift of the Holy Spirit and are added to the kingdom, the church, the body of Christ. So then the one being baptized is in Christ and Christ is in him/her and will wear the name *Christian*. 'The disciples were called Christians first at Antioch.'[5]

Now that one has been baptized into Christ and added to the body of Christ, his church, how does one earn the right to this salvation of which we speak? This is a good place to deal with that question in the event that the thought should

---

[1] Romans 6:3-4, NIV
[2] Galatians 3:27, KJV
[3] Romans 6:5-7, KJV
[4] 2 Corinthians 5:17, KJV
[5] Acts 11:26b, NIV

cross one's mind. The answer is abundantly clear. There is nothing we can do to earn salvation. The price was paid in full when Jesus took upon Himself to pay the debt of sin when He gave his life. Let's hear from the Apostle Paul in his letter to the church at Ephesus. 'But because of his great love for us, God, who is rich in mercy, made us alive with Christ even when we were dead in transgressions—it is by grace you have been saved. And God raised us up with Christ and seated us with him in the heavenly realms in Christ Jesus, in order that in the coming ages he might show the incomparable riches of his grace, expressed in his kindness to us in Christ Jesus. For it is by grace you have been saved, through faith--and this not from yourselves, it is the gift of God—not by works, so no one can boast.'[1] Again the words of Paul: 'For the grace of God that brings salvation has appeared to all men. It teaches us to say no to ungodliness and worldly passions, and to live self-controlled, upright and godly lives in this present age.'[2] We can readily understand then that we can do nothing to earn salvation; it is only by the grace of God that we can be assured of eternal life. Salvation is a gift from God because of his grace offered to all who will embrace it. Notice, too, that Paul told Titus that this grace teaches us also: teaches us what to do and not to do, teaches us the things we need to do to avail ourselves of this grace.

So then, now that we have made entrance into the Kingdom through our obedience to God's will there is nothing left for us to do except wait? This is far from being correct, even though some in the kingdom seem to take this position. It brings to mind a story a preacher once told. A little fellow

---

[1] Ephesians 2:4-9, NIV
[2] Titus 2:11-12, NIV

went to bed at his appointed time, a short time later his parents heard a thud coming from his bedroom. They rushed to see what was going on, and the little fellow was on the floor. When asked what happened he said, "I guess I went to sleep too close to where I got in." Unfortunately it seems some people in the church also go to sleep too close to where they got in. That is just an observation, not a judgment. Salvation is a free gift from God but there are responsibilities that we assume when we become Christians. Let's give this more thought and question ourselves a little further to be certain we fully understand what is required of Christians to remain in the good grace of God.

Chapter Fifteen

In the pages of this writing we have explored some absolutely fascinating facts. Truths the human brain is challenged to comprehend. Have we truly stopped to consider the enormity of what we have been discussing? When we realize how little time we have on this earth and that this should be a time of preparation for the most important thing that can ever be a part of our lives, are we totally concerned? What are our hopes and plans for the future life to come? Have we given due diligence to the teachings of God's word? Is it possible that we have been indifferent to the point that we could let the hope we have slip away? These are questions we should sincerely contemplate as we explore the responsibilities of one who wears the name Christian.

To begin, let's hear the words of Jesus. 'If anyone would come after me, he must deny himself and take up his cross and follow me. For whoever wants to save his life will lose it, but whoever loses his life for me will find it. What good will it be for a man if he gains the whole world, yet forfeits his soul? Or what can a man give in exchange for his soul?'[1] 'And anyone who does not take his cross and follow me is not worthy of me.'[2] So what is Jesus saying? When He says we are to deny ourselves and take up the cross, does that mean that we can literally take up his cross? *No.* Does it mean that we deny ourselves of every pleasure we experience in life? *No.* We cannot bear the actual cross of Christ, but we must be willing to give up anything that separates us from God. Do we deny all pleasure? Certainly not! Consider the pleasures we receive from God's blessings. We have life, our spouse, our parents, our children, our homes, the work we have to support our families, the friends we accrue in our lifetime, the fellow-Christians who share our beliefs. God blesses us with these natural and normal things of life for our good living and pleasure. But, we must never allow anything or anyone on this earth keep us from our responsibilities to God.

The Christians of the first century suffered much for their faith, even being persecuted brutally and put to death. Their belief in God and their faith in the eternity beyond sustained them and gave them courage to stand firm in their allegiance to God. Jesus said if we are not willing to be as dedicated, then we do not deserve Him. Will we as Christians in America be called upon to give our lives for our faith? Probably not too likely, but who knows what might

---

[1] Matthew 16:24-26, NIV
[2] Mat 10:38, NIV

happen? The more important question is: Will we be willing to do so if such a situation presents itself? In other parts of the world it happens frequently.

Peter said, speaking of Christians: 'But you are a chosen people, a royal priesthood, a holy nation, a people belonging to God, that you may declare the praises of him who called you out of darkness into his wonderful light.'[1] Jesus said: 'You are the light of the world. A city on a hill cannot be hidden. Neither do people light a lamp and put it under a bowl, instead they put it on its stand, and it gives light to everyone in the house. In the same way, let your light shine before men, that they may see your good deeds and praise your father in heaven.'[2] Do these thoughts portray what people see in us as children of God? Christians are a chosen people, chosen by the word of God, a holy nation that should show our faith by the life we live and praise Him who brought us out of sin into the kingdom of his dear Son. Does the life we live reflect this? Do we worship the God that gives us hope? Do we praise his name and give to Him the glory in all we do? 'But the hour cometh, and now is, when the true worshippers shall worship the Father in spirit and in truth: for the Father seeketh such to worship him. God is a spirit and they that worship him must worship him in spirit and in truth.'[3] How do we view this in comparison to our dedication?

An excellent thing to do would be to take the time to go back into the Old Testament and re-read Exodus, Leviticus and Numbers. Those people of God who had been rescued from Egyptian slavery were given very specific instructions

[1] 1 Peter 2:9, NIV
[2] Matthew 5:14-15, NIV
[3] John 4:23-24, KJV

of how they were to serve God. The manner of dress for the Priests, the making of the tabernacle, the creation of the tools used in the sacrifices, detailed instructions for every facet of their service. We will not belabor the point, but know that God's requirements for them were exacting and they were required to adhere to every facet without fail. We know that God dealt harshly with Israel when they failed to meet his instructions. Does this give us pause to consider our service to Him? Remember also that through their sacrifices there was no forgiveness of sins. Only a yearly remembrance: 'for it is not possible that the blood of bulls and goats should take away sins.'[1] When we realize the requirements incumbent on those people does it make us question our dedication?

The writer of the Hebrew letter said: 'Let us not give up meeting together, as some are in the habit of doing, but let us encourage one another—and all the more as you see the Day approaching.'[2] How do we react to these words from the Scriptures? When we truly do some soul-searching, in total honesty with ourselves, can we say we are faithful in our worship? We know from the Scriptures that the early church met on the first day of the week. They met to worship, to break bread in remembrance of the sacrifice of the Savior. Should we do any less today? Perhaps it would be better to ask, *do we dare do any less?* We are not given a lot of information about their services, so we don't know if it was for hours, all day, all day and all night. We do know that the Apostle Paul preached at Troas once until midnight.[3] Many today want to devote an hour on Sunday

---

[1] Hebrews 10:4, KJV
[2] Hebrews 10:25, NIV
[3] Acts 20

morning only if there is nothing we think is more important. Do we ever wonder how God views this?

There are no Scriptures that instruct us to meet again on Sunday evening or even for a midweek service. However, if the leadership of a congregation deems it wise and necessary, should we not participate? It seems reasonable to think that if there are two hundred people on Sunday morning for worship, there should be two hundred in the evening service. If we intend to please God, and our hopes are in Him to provide a life in eternity, why would we not want to be present at all services? If we don't feel like giving a few hours each week to God, why would we want an eternity with Him? If there is nothing in this life that is more important than preparing for eternal life, how can we let other activities keep us from church service where we worship and honor the God who has given to us a way of salvation and eternal bliss? Not a judgment, just a thought.

Then let's give some thought to the communion service, a memorial to the suffering and death of our Savior. This is an act of remembrance of Christ's suffering and death, which He instituted and told us as often as we do this we do it in remembrance of Him.[1] As we partake of the communion our thoughts should be on nothing other than Christ and his suffering and death. The Lord's Supper, as we often call it, is a monument to the Christ that bought our freedom with his blood. He suffered brutally on the cross. He did for us what we could never do for ourselves. Is He not worthy of this monument? There is no time as sacred as the time we spend at the Lord's Table. As we prepare ourselves to partake of the symbols of his love let us remember his

---

[1] Matthew 26:26-28, Mark 14:22-24, Luke 22:19-20, 1 Corinthians 11:23-26

words: "Do this in remembrance of me" and let nothing interfere with this part of our worship. Let us think on these things soberly and prayerfully. We will touch briefly on a few more thoughts and bring this writing to an end.

Chapter Sixteen

As stated in the beginning, there is nothing in this writing
that is judgmental, argumentative or cause for debate. Chal-
lenging? Yes, it is hoped that we all will be challenged to
take a long hard look at the truths that have been set forth,
then take another long hard look at how we react to these
truths. To live the Christian life is demanding. It requires
that at certain times and in some ways we must make sacrifices. Are we really giving up anything? In most cases the
answer would be no, especially when we realize how often
we do not distinguish between our needs and our wants.
We must focus on those things which are meaningful and
essential and center our lives on the promises of our God.
Peter said his promises are exceeding great and precious.[1]

---

[1] 2 Peter 1:4

The promise of Christ dwelling in us and we dwelling in Christ, the promise of eternal life to the faithful, these are the great and precious promises. In fact it is our only hope. Paul said that Christ in us is our hope for glory.[1]

So then, as we seek to serve God, is it not reasonable that we look at our practices, question ourselves from time to time? 'Upon the first day of the week let every one of you lay by him in store, as God hath prospered him, that there be no gathering when I come.'[2] When we are making plans for our contribution to the church, do we really think things through and give as we have been prospered? Are we being honest with ourselves and with God? And dare we be otherwise? 'But this I say, he which soweth sparingly shall reap also sparingly; and he which soweth bountifully shall reap also bountifully. Every man according as he purposeth in his heart, so let him give; not grudgingly, or of necessity: for God loveth a cheerful giver.'[3] We might do well to ask ourselves how we think God views our contribution.

What about our prayer life? 'Rejoice evermore, pray without ceasing. In everything give thanks: for this is the will of God in Christ Jesus concerning you.'[4] God is the source of all our blessings and for each and every blessing we should rejoice and be thankful that we have been afforded prayer as a means of communing with the Father. 'Let us therefore come boldly unto the throne of grace, that we may obtain mercy, and find grace to help in time of need.'[5] What a wondrous privilege it is that we can go to the Father to seek

---

[1] Colossians 1:27b
[2] 1 Corinthians 16:2, KJV
[3] 2 Corinthians 9:6-7, KJV
[4] 1 Thessalonians 5:16-18, KJV
[5] Hebrews 4:16, KJV

comfort and strength and know He is there for us! 'And we are confident that he hears us whenever we ask for anything that pleases Him. And since we know He hears us when we make our requests, we also know that He will give us what we ask for.'[1] The Apostle Paul counseled the Christians at Colossae: 'Devote yourselves to prayer with an alert mind and a thankful heart.'[2] James tells us: 'Confess your sins to each other and pray for each other so that you may be healed. The earnest prayer of a righteous person has great power and produces wonderful results.'[3] God is the source of each and every blessing we enjoy, and these blessings are innumerable. Prayer is one of the privileges we have as his children. Can we say we are diligent and consistent with our prayer life?

Another thought relevant to our study at this point: How much time do we spend reading and studying the Bible? How will we know how to conduct our lives if we do not heed God's teaching? 'Study to show thyself approved unto God, a workman that needeth not to be ashamed, rightly dividing the word of truth.'[4] It is needful that we contemplate these things in order that we do not miss out on the eternal joy that God has made available to us. We must be persistent in our service to God and studying and knowing his word is most important. Without a knowledge of his will which we gain through study, we can lose our way. The writer of the Hebrew letter warned the Christians to whom he was writing. 'Let us therefore fear, lest, a promise being left us of entering into his rest, any of you should

---

[1] 1 John 5:14-15, NLT
[2] Colossians 4:2, NLT
[3] James 5:16, NLT
[4] 2 Timothy 2:15, KJV

seem to come short of it.'[1] Paul also warned: 'Wherefore
let him that thinketh he standeth take heed lest he fall.'[2]
The possibility of missing out on eternal life in God's presence is unthinkable, but entirely possible. Only through a
knowledge of God's word will we find strength and courage to live as He wishes. We as Christians have an enemy,
an adversary that wishes to separate us from God. He
would like nothing more than to see us let sin overcome us.
We have to be knowledgeable and wary of being overcome
with sin and separated again from God. 'Be sober, be vigilant; because your adversary the devil, as a roaring lion,
walketh about, seeking whom he may devour.'[3]

Sin, any sin of which we have not repented will separate us
from God. John says: 'If we say that we have fellowship
with him, and walk in darkness, we lie, and do not the
truth.'[4] As human beings we all sin. Hear again the words
of John: 'My little children, these things I write unto you
that ye sin not. And if any man sin, we have an advocate
with the father, Jesus Christ the righteous. And he is the
propitiation for our sins; and not for ours only, but also for
the sins of the whole world.'[5] Jesus paid the price for our
sins, and He will be the one who speaks to God in our de-
fense. These are words of comfort to the Christian. There is
no reason for any Christian to be burdened with sin. Jesus
is the propitiation for our sins, He paid the price. Jesus is
our spokesman before God. He knew temptation, hunger,
pain and rejection and can speak for us to the Father. And
more than this, his blood will continually cleanse us from

---

[1] Hebrews 4:1, KJV
[2] I Corinthians 10:12, KJV
[3] 1 Peter 5:8, KJV
[4] 1 John 1:6, KJV
[5] 1 John 2:1-2, KJV

sin if we allow it. 'But if we walk in the light as he is in the light, we have fellowship one with another, and the blood of Jesus Christ his Son cleanseth us from all sin.'[1] The Greek word used here for *cleanseth* is *katharizo.* Used in the present tense, this word means that the blood of Christ is continually available to absolve us from the defilement of sin. We understand that as human beings we are not without sin in our lives. We realize that sin separates us from God and in that condition we are lost, but when we repent and ask, his blood will clean and restore us to God. What could give us greater peace of mind than these truths from God's word?

---

[1] 1 John 1:7, KJV

Chapter Seventeen

In his poem, *Maud Muller*, John Greenleaf Whittier relates the story of a sweet-spirited and pretty farm lass who had an encounter with a Judge who was riding by and stopped to ask for a drink of water. In her tattered dress and bare feet, to the Judge she was one to be admired. He in his fine clothes was from a different world than hers, but she pondered what it might be to live the life he did. They were smitten with each other, but the Judge rode on. He married into wealth and position; she married a farmer and had a life of want. Both the Judge and Maud were haunted by the feelings they had from the encounter: He in an unhappy marriage and she the life of a drudge. In the final verse of the poem, we find these poignant words: 'For of all sad words of tongue or pen, the saddest are these, it might have been.' In the realm of pathos, the story elicits a feeling of heartache and yearning for what could have been. People are continually reminded of what might have been, but facing the reality of what is.

Do these same thoughts come to our mind on occasion? Perhaps we have veered off the pathway, taken the wrong course, chapters in our life we would like to delete? Most likely this fits most of us. It is indeed a saddening thought, if we are not where we want to be, to think about what might have been. What could have been? No doubt the rich man in Christ's story who dressed in purple and fine linens and fared sumptuously thought about what might have been. He died and was in torment.[1] He looked across the chasm where he saw the beggar Lazarus who was in the presence of Abraham and was comforted. The rich man begged for concessions for himself and his brothers but was denied. It was too late. Whatever is to be done must be done while we are living on this earth. There will be no other opportunities to change course. When we stop to think of the provisions God has made for us to dwell in his realm for all of time that will be unending, how can we not be concerned with our way of life? Giving thought to this, what can we imagine of anything related to this life that is of more importance than eternal life in the heavenly realm?

In the Revelation of John, we read of three congregations of the children of God. John was instructed by the Lord to write to seven churches and was told what he was to say to them, but we will concentrate on three in particular. To the church at Philadelphia: 'I know your deeds, see, I have placed before you an open door that no one can shut. I know that you have little strength, yet you have kept my word and have not denied my name.' 'Since you have kept

---

[1] Luke 16:19-31

my command to endure patiently, I will also keep you from the hour of trial that is going to come upon the whole world to test those who live on earth.'[1] We get a view of a church that was doing its best to live by the teachings of the Lord. He was pleased with those people and promised to be with them in any time of trial or duress. This was not to say there would not be bad situations presenting themselves. But, rather, that with his help they would be able to withstand any trials and be victorious. What more could any congregation of the Lord's people desire than to be recognized as determined and steady and abiding in his word?

To the church at Sardis: 'I know your deeds; you have a reputation of being alive, but you are dead. Wake up! Strengthen what remains and is about to die, for I have not found your deeds complete in the sight of my God.'[2] This assessment of that church should have frightened them into action to make themselves right. He said they were recognized in his sight as being dead but at least with hope. He told them to wake up and get back on track and to do so before it was too late.

To the church at Laodicea: 'I know all the things you do, that you are neither hot nor cold. I wish that you were one or the other. But since you are like lukewarm water, neither hot nor cold, I will spit you out of my mouth. You say, I am rich. I have everything I want, I don't need a thing. And you don't realize that you are wretched and miserable and poor and blind and naked.'[3] Were they beyond hope? In their present condition they were without hope. Christ said they were an abomination and worthy of being cast away,

---

[1] Revelation 3:8, 10, NIV
[2] Revelation 3:1-2, NIV
[3] Revelation 3"15-17, NLT

but while they were alive, they could change. One might wonder why Christ would say they were worthy of being spit out? If they were fervent, they would be diligent in the work of the church. If they were absolutely cold, they were separate and apart from God. Being lukewarm perhaps they were doing more damage to the church, not any better than those who never embraced and obeyed the word of God. In any case, it would be the absolute worst thing that could happen, to be cast away from the Lord.

'Watch out that you do not lose what you have worked for, but that you may be rewarded fully.'[1] What is John telling us in these words of caution? Three thoughts come to mind. One: that it is certainly possible for one to lose the reward which we seek. Two: that it is important for us to be diligent, always examining ourselves to be certain we are living as we should. Three: that we be constantly on guard for the temptations that are put before us. Let's hear Peter again: 'Be sober, be vigilant; because your adversary the devil, as a roaring lion, walketh about, seeking whom he may devour.'[2] We cannot be reminded of this too often. We each must acknowledge certain facts that are undeniable. Life is short: death, the resurrection, the judgment and eternal life or eternal condemnation awaits all. Let us dwell on these truths that will give us direction in life. Believe in God's promises and live in such a manner that we look forward to hearing Him say, 'Well done, thou good and faithful servant, enter into my rest.' This is his desire and hope for all. 'Believest thou this?'

---

[1] 2 John 8, NIV
[2] 1 Peter 5:8, KJV

Epilogue

The stage lights are slowly dimmed as the curtain is drawn for the last time. The star of the show has taken his final bow. The house lights are brought up as the audience leave their seats and boxes and slowly proceed to the exits. Those in attendance are generous with their comments about their perception of what has just been played out before them. Some express positive thoughts; others have questions or doubts about the enactment, while still others ponder in their minds the true meaning of what they have witnessed.

Was this a Broadway show, perhaps an off-Broadway production? Maybe it was the home town little theatre group or the Senior High School class play. It is possible that it could have been any one of those, but it wasn't.

To paraphrase Shakespeare, the stage was the world, and the lead actor was one of us. It was a portrayal of the inevitable in which each of us will play our part. We will all come to that point in this life when we are on the stage for the last time. As we finish our play, and the curtain is coming down, we will pass beyond the vale of this life and proceed to the next. We each were given a play-book that contained all the lines and all the moves. The outcome of our part will be in keeping with effort we put into the play. We will then await the revue of our effort. There will only be one critic with whom we will be concerned. Only one revue will matter.

When we come into this life, we have a certain amount of time to be alive on this planet. How much time is that? We simply do not know. It could be just a few years, or it could possibly be a century. We are not allowed to know the time we will be allotted. It is a certainty that each of us will reach that point sooner or later that we make our final appearance, our final act. There is nothing morbid about these thoughts; it is just a reality we each face. Do we think of this with trepidation, or do we face it with assurance and a yearning to learn what lies ahead? It depends on the course we have chosen. To the child of God, death has no sting; death has no victory.

The final verse of William Cullen Bryant's Thanatopsis has so much meaning we will include it here as we bring this writing to an end.

So live that when thy summons comes to join the innumerable caravan that moves to that mysterious realm, where each shall take his chamber in the silent halls of death, thou go not, like the quarry slave at night, scourged to his dungeon, but, sustained and soothed by an unfaltering trust, approach thy grave like one who wraps the drapery of his couch about him, and lies down to pleasant dreams.